YORK'S
AIRPORTS

CONTENTS

NEW YORK'S AIRPORTS

John F. Kennedy • Newark • LaGuardia

Aram Gesar

Motorbooks International
Publishers & Wholesalers ®

Author's Note

Landing in New York's Kennedy airport is one of the most exciting travel memories I have. It was early July of 1970 during a very hot summer afternoon, on a Pan Am 747-121 inbound from London's Heathrow. I was very excited because it was my first Atlantic crossing and landing in the United States. Our flight had a delay of four hours in London, but it did not matter thanks to my enthusiasm, it was my first flight on board the 747, at that time still having engine problems encountered in its first year of service.

Nothing compares to the air traffic encountered in the New York area. During the course of one year, there are over one million aircraft movements in this relatively small airspace. Nowhere else have I seen such a range of modern and old airport infrastructures, and such a mixture of aircraft ranging from the supersonic Concorde, seen up to five times a day, to the latest Airbus A340, Boeing 747-400 or the rare Russian IL-62 or IL-86, all flying among the shorter range workhorses such as the DC-9, MD-80, 737 and commuter aircraft.

The presence of business aircraft is also very substantial ranging from the small Learjets to large presidential 747s plus the full range of Falcons, Gulfstreams and modified airliners such as the 707, 737 and the very popular, among the private jetset, the 727.

During the preparation of this book, I have been fortunate to receive help and advice from people associated with New York's Kennedy, Newark and LaGuardia airports. I thank everyone who has answered our requests for access to the airports, aircraft and information so patiently. Everyone I came into contact with was most helpful, but I would particularly like to express my gratitude to the staff of Port Authority of New York & New Jersey: Pete Florio, Jack Gartner, Frank Huer, John Jacoby, David Kaufman, Dan Keough, Frank Lopano, David Plavin, Bradley Rubenstein, and flight crews and ground personnel of American Airlines, Air France, Balair, British Airways, Island & New York Helicopter, Japan Airlines, Swissair, Trans World Airlines.

Aram Gesar

This edition first published in 1994 by Motorbooks International, Publishers & Wholesalers, PO Box 2, 729 Prospect Avenue, Osceola, WI 54020, USA.

Copyright © 1994 Pyramid Media Group, New York.

Previously published in the UK in 1994 by Airlife Publishing Ltd.

Motorbooks International books are also available at discounts in bulk quantity for industrial sales-promotional use. For details write to Special Sales Manager at the publisher's address.

Library of Congress Cataloging-in-Publication Data
ISBN 0-87938-901-X

Text by Aram Gesar.

Edited by David Quast.

All photographs:
Copyright © 1977-93 Aram Gesar
Except on pages:
Frank Loprano: 81, 89, 93.
Port Authority of NY and NJ: 6, 7, 8, 74, 94, 95, 114, 116, 118.

A Book Edited and Produced by Pyramid Media Group, 420 Lexington Avenue, Room 445, New York, NY 10170.

Electronic Production by Suzanne Reitwiesner.

Printed and bound in Hong Kong.

Foreword

The three-airport system comprised of John F. Kennedy International (JFK), Newark International (EWR) and LaGuardia (LGA) airports, is the major air transportation hub for the New York/New Jersey region and one of the busiest airport systems in the world, handling more passengers, more flights and more air cargo than any other airport system.

Each of our airports is steeped in aviation history. By the time EWR became the world's busiest commercial airport in 1937, it had already accrued a list of aviation firsts including the first airport weather bureau, paved runway, night lighting and air traffic control. During the years of World War II, the airport was operated by the U.S. Army and was the stateside jumping-off point for thousands of aircraft bound for the overseas theaters of war. Following substantial redevelopment in the '70s, EWR became the hub for People Express, one of the first of the no-frills airlines that took advantage of a deregulated industry and helped make air travel accessible to an expanded market of travelers.

LGA came into being largely through the efforts of its namesake and most enthusiastic advocate, New York City Mayor Fiorello LaGuardia. He maintained that New York City, as one of the world's great cities, should have its own airport and not rely on nearby EWR for its air service. A decorated World War I bomber squadron leader, LaGuardia realized the importance of aviation and its potential to the growth and commerce of the entire New York region. His persistence led the effort that resulted in the opening in 1939 of New York Municipal Airport, which was shortly thereafter renamed in honor of its most dedicated champion. LGA was soon vying with EWR for flight activity from the major airlines of the day — Eastern, Trans World, American, United and many of the fledgling airlines that would grow and prosper as the aviation industry did the same. LGA also became the home of the great Pan American Clippers, "flying boats" that crossed the Atlantic. These first giants of the air used the waterways for runways and offered their passengers dining accommodations and sleeping rooms that rivaled the luxuries of the steamship lines, but with a much quicker ocean crossing.

JFK reflects the post World War II growth of the aviation industry. Started in 1942 on the grounds of the former Idlewild Golf Course and adding to its length and breadth with recovered marshland, JFK began as a New York City project. The great bombers and cargo carriers developed for war would find peacetime use there as air passenger and cargo aircraft. These new members of the airline fleets had longer ranges and greater capacities, which required larger airports with more terminal space, longer runways and many additional ground service facilities. Airports also needed to accommodate the growing number of foreign flag carriers and to replace the great passenger ship terminals as the principal international gateways for visitors and immigrants alike. Called New York International Airport when it was opened in 1948, the airport was officially renamed in honor of the late President Kennedy in December, 1963. The first of its terminals, completed in 1957, was the International Arrivals Building and throughout the late '50s into the '60s Terminal City grew into a ring of eight more major unit air terminal buildings. Today the airport serves nearly 100 domestic and foreign flag airlines.

Each of the three airports was established as a project of its respective city. In 1948 they all were turned over to The Port Authority of New York and New Jersey through lease agreements with Newark and New York City. The Port Authority was charged with the operation, maintenance and development of the three airports, relieving the cities and their residents of what had become a substantial tax burden. With this change the airports became a system, acting in concert rather than in competition. Recent analysis shows that the system contributes $22.2 billion annually to the economy of the New York/New Jersey region.

We continue to grow, keeping pace with an industry where technological advances in the full range of related fields occur in the blink of an eye. And we continue to strive to serve the ultimate consumer, the air passenger, with as many services on the ground as the aircraft manufacturers and airlines provide in the skies.

A new round of major redevelopment programs has been under way at our airports since the late 1980s and will continue into the next century. At LGA the Central Terminal Building has been expanded and modernized, USAir has built a modern new terminal, the roadway system has been upgraded and improved and many of the airport's utilities and other systems are being modernized. At EWR a monorail system connecting all the terminals will open at the end of 1994, a new international arrivals facility is under construction, roadways and service roads are being upgraded, terminal frontages are being upgraded and cargo facilities are being expanded. At JFK a new Air Traffic Control tower enters operation this year, the entire airport roadway system is being revised and improved, a major rehabilitation of the International Arrivals Building has been completed, a new parking garage has been built, utilities have been modernized and many other rehabilitation projects are under way.

It is an exciting time in aviation, as much for the developments on the ground as those in the air. We hope that you will come and share the excitement with us. Visit us and see what's been done so far, what's being done right now, and watch for what is yet to come.

David Z. Plavin, Director of Aviation,
The Port Authority of New York and New Jersey

John F. Kennedy International

New York's international airport was originally known by the name Idlewild, the complex was designed to become twice the size of LaGuardia, and with the availability of seven runways, it was expected to handle 1,000 movements per day. Construction began in April, 1942, when city authorities were contracted to fill the marshy tidelands on the site of Idlewild Golf Course.

After much delay, commercial flying began on July 1, 1948, followed 30 days later by the official opening. The first scheduled airline flight into the airport was made by Peruvian International Airways on July 9. By this time the airport had adopted the title of New York International and was under the control of the Port Authority of New York and New Jersey.

The airport location was some 15 miles by highway from midtown Manhattan, in the southeastern section of the borough of Queens. Original plans called for a 1,000 acre airport. Today the airport covers almost 5,000 acres (with 840 acres devoted to the Central Terminal Area alone)—equivalent in size of all of Manhattan from 42nd Street south to the Battery. Original construction amounted to $60 million. By 1983 the Port Authority had invested $770 million at the airport. The runway system consists now of two pairs of parallel runways.

An elliptical center area was allocated to the terminal buildings, although those erected in the early days were intended to be a temporary expedient to enable operations to begin. After hangars and a new 10-story air traffic control tower were completed in the early 1950s, attention was given to permanent structures for passenger handling. An International Arrivals complex was created in the center of the airport with two adjoining east and west wings, surrounded by a dual ring of peripheral taxiways. It was opened in 1958. Initially 655 acres, its area was enlarged to 840 acres by relocation of taxiways to provide space needed for expansion of the passenger terminals. There are now about 178 aircraft gate positions serving the various terminals.

The remainder of the individual terminals was allocated to specific airlines. They became responsible for the design of their own premises, leading to a wide variation of styles. Originally the Eastern Air Lines Terminal, Terminal One opened in 1956, United and Pan American each opened a terminal in 1960 and American in 1961. In 1962, Trans World Airlines and Northwest opened terminals. Later National Airlines opened a terminal in 1969 and British Airways in 1970.

Through the years the center area has been expanded considerably despite the limitations of expanding the facility beyond its present perimeter. Inevitably some of the runways were sacrificed, leaving two pairs of parallel main strips plus a fifth for the use of general aviation aircraft. With the southern perimeter bordered by Jamaica Bay, the only prospect for more expansion

was to reclaim additional land from the sea.

Even by the mid-1960s, John F. Kennedy, as it was renamed in December, 1963, following the assassination of the President in Dallas, was handling an enormous amount of air cargo. It already possessed the world's largest freight center, but plans were made to increase the area significantly and give it better road access.

In the late 1980s a major development program began at JFK, first involving construction of the new 30 story Air Traffic Control Tower. The new completed tower which soars 321 feet, and is the tallest in North America provides controllers with unobstructed views of the entire aeronautical area and the FAA is installing state-of-the-art communications, radar and windshear alert systems. Located on the ramp side of the International Arrivals complex, it become operational in 1991. Ramp control opened in 1993. Studies have also begun into the feasibility of a rail link to connect the terminals with the Long Island Rail Road and New York City subway system at Jamaica station in Queens. An extension of the track to LaGuardia is also being considered.

In 1992, 35,800 people were employed at JFK, down from 40,300 the year before, and well below the peak of 44,500 in 1984. Kennedy Airport officials are making

plans for major changes in the future. Already the home of more than 100 airlines in 1991, eight new carriers were added in 1992. Construction of a Cogeneration Plant began in May, 1992. The facility will generate both electric power and thermal energy for the airport and help relieve the overburdened power systems of the neighboring communities.

In 1991, British Airways completed a $120 million expansion of its terminal, which opened in 1970. United Airlines is a joint tenant with six gates in the modernized British terminal. American Airlines also completed a $115 million renovation and constructed a connector between its terminal and Terminal Three (the former United Terminal). Pan Am had expanded into the adjacent former Northwest Terminal and built a connector pedestrian walk. In November 1991, Delta Air Lines assumed many of its routes and both of its terminals, now called Delta Flight Center and Terminal 1A.

A consortium of foreign flag carriers—Air France, Japan Airlines, Korean Air and Lufthansa—was formed to build a new international terminal on the site of Terminal One, the former Eastern Airlines terminal. Construction is beginning in early 1994 on this, the first new terminal at JFK in more than 20 years.

Aircraft rescue and fire-fighting operations were enhanced by the opening of the new Satellite Rescue Station, located between Runways 22R and 22L. The new structure covers 21,000 square feet. The facility has five garage bays to house emergency vehicles used during aircraft incidents at JFK.

A new airport road system is under construction. New roads opened in 1992 allow access to three of the quadrants into which the central terminal area will be divided. Access to the fourth quadrant will be established in 1993. In 1992 the U.S.

Federal Aviation Administration approved a plan by the Port Authority of New York and New Jersey to begin collecting $282 million in Passenger Facility Charges at Kennedy, LaGuardia and Newark airports effective Oct. 1, 1992. The approval included authority to spend $21 million for planning, environmental and other studies for proposed transit links at all three airports.

Terminal One opened in 1956, United, American and Pan American each opened a terminal in 1960. In 1962, Trans World Airlines and Northwest opened terminals.

Through the years the center area has been expanded considerably despite the limitations of expanding the facility beyond its present perimeter. Inevitably some of the runways were sacrificed, leaving two pairs of parallel main strips plus a fifth for the use of general aviation aircraft. With the southern perimeter bordered by Jamaica Bay, the only prospect for more expansion was to reclaim additional land from the sea. Even by the mid-1960s, John F. Kennedy, as it was renamed in December, 1963, following the assassination of the President in Dallas, was handling an enormous amount of air cargo. It already possessed the world's largest freight center, but plans were made to increase the area significantly and give it better road access.

In the late 1980s a major development program began at JFK, first involving construction of the new 30 storey Air Traffic Control Tower, which soars 321 feet, and is the tallest in North America, will provide controllers with unobstructed views of the entire aeronautical area.

The FAA installed state-of-the-art communications, radar and windshear alert sys-

tems. Located on the ramp side of the International Arrivals complex, it became operational in 1991.

A new $3-million General Aviation Terminal was built in 1993. The 14,000-square-foot terminal is part of Japan Airlines Management Corp.'s redevelopment of Building 14 into a major center for its U.S. operations

John F. Kennedy International Airport is shown from the air. The airport now covers an area the size of Manhattan from 42nd Street south to the Battery. Originally the site of Idlewild Golf Course, the present airport has run out of land on which to expand. Future expansion can be made only by producing landfill for Jamaica Bay, which is a bird sanctuary. Aerial view of the airport shows a series of small single unit terminals eventually forming a circle. Individual airlines or groups of airlines operate their own terminals, with a variety of architectural styles.

In the foreground are the terminal originally built for Pan American World Airways and Runway 13R/31L. The terminal now is leased by Delta Air Lines. Delta intends to invest $150 million in the renovation of its two terminals, Terminal 1A and the Delta Flight Center. In 1992 Delta was the third largest carrier at JFK, carrying 2.8 million passengers—almost 10% of the total number of passengers carried at the airport that year.

Pan American inaugurated jet service with the Boeing 707 on the New York-Paris route in 1958. Pan Am had placed the launching order for the aircraft on Oct. 13, 1955, more than three years after the De Havilland Comet had become the world's first jet airliner in service. Pan Am also was the first airline to fly the 747 jumbo jet from this terminal to London in 1970. Boeing built 917 Model 707s, excluding airframes for the E-3 and E-6 military programs.

The view from the roof parking area clearly shows the aircraft docked at the gates and the taxi and runway traffic on Runway 13R/31L. In 1992 Kennedy International recorded 4.4 million paid parked cars at the airport, down only slightly from the 4.6 million at the airport in 1979. Airport officials are expanding public transportation to and from the airport, due to the glut of automobiles and lack of space for expanding parking areas. Snow and ice often accumulates on Runway 13R/31L. New de-icing procedures have been introduced at the airport.

A Boeing 707-320B of Avianca landing in 1977.
The 707 aircraft operated by this airline were manufactured originally for other airlines including several 707-320B and -320C built for Pan Am. The airline
also flies 747-200 and 767-200ER aircraft to
Kennedy.

A Russian built Il-62M operated for Air Ukraine can be seen at gates at the Delta Air Lines terminal. The Ilyushin Il-62M had rear-mounted engines, similar to the engine placement on the British VC-10. The Il-62 first flew in 1963 and entered service with Aeroflot later in the 1960s, providing long-haul service. The Il-62 required lengthy flight development to overcome the tendency of this aircraft type to enter a deep stall from which recovery was impossible.

A Russian Aeroflot Il-86 is taking off. This aircraft was the first wide-body aircraft manufactured in the former USSR. It was also the first Russian airliner to have its engines in wing mounted pods, rather than rear-mounted on the fuselage or buried in the wing roots. A new registration code and the flag of Russia replace the red communist flag.

The engines of the Il-86 are not very efficient. When flying westbound over the Atlantic the aircraft often must refuel at Gander if the winds are strong. An interesting feature of the aircraft is that entry to the cabin is by way of airstairs that are incorporated in three doors at ground level in the lower fuselage. From the lower deck vestibules, where heavy winter coats can be stowed, stairs lead up to the main cabin, making the aircraft independent of airport loading stairs.

Most of the Airbus Industrie A310 aircraft operated by Delta at Kennedy formerly belonged to Pan Am. The airline liked the aircraft so much it ordered its own A310-300s. Delta uses A310-300 and -200 transports to fly to European capitals. The extended-range version of the A310, the -300, has small wingtip fences and tailplane tank to increase fuel capacity. Wingtip fences reduce drag and improve lateral control. Originally on the -300 only, now it is on all A310 aircraft. An A310 requires 7,500 ft. (2,300 m.) of runway for takeoff and a speed of 165 mph. (192 kph.), about 30% less than a large trijet or a 747.

Singapore Airlines 747-400 is parked near the Delta Air Lines terminal. Boeing launched the 747-400 in October, 1985, on the basis of an order for 10 aircraft placed by Northwest Airlines; this was followed by a 14-aircraft order from Singapore Airlines in March, 1986. Swissair and Singapore are part of the global partnership with Delta. With this aircraft, 10 to 14-hour flights have become routine.

An Alitalia 747-200 taxies near Runway 13R/31L, on its way to departure.
The three metal structures are the Federal Aviation Administration transmitter
towers. The -200 version was first flown on Oct. 11, 1970. It differed from
the -100 in that it had increased weight, carried more fuel and used uprated
engines. Versions of the 747-200 were developed as pure freighter (Model
747F) or convertible passenger/freighter (Model 747C) aircraft, with upward-
hinged nose for straight-in freight loading.

A DC-8-62 of Nationair of Quebec, Canada taking off on runway 13R. The air-line operated -61 and -63 aircraft as well as 757 and 747 aircraft, the DC-8 as equipped with "hush kits" on their engines to apply to the new low-noise rules introduced in all U.S. airports. Its Pratt & Whitney JT3D turbofan engines are the DC-8 original powerplant type.

Taxiing along Runways 13R/31L a
Fokker F28 and a United 767-200, just
before take off.

An Air China 747-200 taxiing along runways 13R/31L prior to takeoff. The Boeing 747-300 series or advanced models of the -200 weighs, on average, 383,000 lb. (174,000 kg.) when empty. It can lift 833,000 lb. (378,600 kg.). The difference is made up of fuel, provisions, passengers, their luggage and cargo. The cockpit crew is busy doing last-minute checks on equipment and talking to the control tower, awaiting clearances to move ahead to the next step in the process.

on activity near the Delta terminal and the intersection of Runway
/31L and 4L/22R, picture taken prior to Delta takeover of Pan Am.
nedy Airport's International terminal symbolizes JFK as the gateway to
world. In 1992 the airport had almost 322,000 aircraft movements—
000 of which were domestic. Of foreign destinations for passengers
arting Kennedy in 1991, the top 10 were London, Paris, Frankfurt, Rome,
vo, Amsterdam, Madrid, Brussels, Shannon and Tel Aviv.

DC-10-15 of Mexicana is shown near the airport's International Terminal. This "hot and high" version of the basic DC-10-10 had a more powerful General Electric CF6-50 engines. A total of 380 DC-10s were built.

A Lufthansa DC-10-30 takes off from Runway 22R, the airline no longer operates the aircraft. Runway 4L/22R intersects with Runway 13R/31L. This version of the basic DC-10-10 had a wingspan increased from 155 ft. to 165 ft.,
much greater fuel capacity, an extra twin-wheel main gear on the centerline,
and new General Electric twin engines in the 50,000 lb. class. A total of 380
DC-10s were built.

A 747-200 is shown on its way to the International terminal. Air France operates 747-200 and -400 to Kennedy, Royal Jordanian provides Lockheed L1011-500 service, just like the one seen at the gate to the right of the 747. These aircraft have a daily utilization rate of more than 10 hours. The basic 747 has room for six galleys, 16 toilets, 6,190 cu. ft. of cargo and baggage space, and 146 survival suits carried as part of the emergency equipment on polar flights.

Korean Air has flown all types of 747s to Kennedy, this one is a 747-400. The aircraft dock at gates. Here they are refueled and receive ordinary maintenance. Electric power is provided. Provisions for the passengers are available. Fueling at Kennedy airport can be accomplished by trucks accessing underground fuel depots. Fuel measurement is an important exercise. It affects the weight of the aircraft and its range. Fuel usage is one of the issues of nearly constant monitoring in the cockpit.

Crew is shown in the cockpit of a CSA
Czechoslovak Airlines A310-300. The cockpit
developed for the A310 has been incorporated in the A300-600. The A310-300 was
developed with a tailplane trim tank to
increase fuel capacity, as well as optional
underfloor tanks, in an effort to extend the
range of the basic aircraft.

A Swissair 747-300 is landing on Runway 22R on the left of the row of 747s parked on the apron for pre-flight preparations across from the International terminal. Wide-body traffic during the afternoon can be intense. The rush hour starts at 3 p.m. and lasts until about 8 p.m. In designing terminal space, aircraft developers determined the size of the space by estimating the number of passengers arriving and departing during peak hours, then multiplied that figure by four, to allow for friends and relatives.

Northwest 747-400 taking off with its wings bending due to the full load on board the aircraft flying to Tokyo non-stop. The airline was the launch customer for the -400 powered with Pratt & Whitney PW4000 series engines.

DC-10-30 of Spanish charter airline Spantax distorted by the summer heat. The company bought ex-Swissair DC-10-30s and Convair CV990s. Spantax went out of business in 1988.

Air France parks a back-up Concorde across from its gate at the International terminal. The aircraft are rotated every day. Concorde's tail contains a fuel tank. In supersonic flight, that fuel helps keep the nose high. The aircraft underwent more than 5,000 hours of wind tunnel tests to prove that the long, streamlined fuselage and slender ogival delta wings would provide good control at speeds as low as 230 mph. with a low drag up to 1,350 mph. (Mach 2).

View is of the interior of the TWA international terminal prior to the rush hour for international departures. There can be a deceptively calm appearance inside the terminal prior to the rush hour for international departures. A 747-200 is at the gate waiting for its passengers. Just over 15 million passengers departed for international destinations in 1992, up from about 14.5 million the previous year. The biggest year for numbers of international passengers departing from JFK was 1988, when 16.7 million people flew out of the airport headed for non-U.S. destinations.

A TWA 767-200 taxiing to a gates on the north side of the TWA international terminal. The airline converted all its -200 to the ER configuration for long range Transatlantic service. An important element among the precautions required for extended range flight is experience of a flight crew with a particular engine and airframe combination. The 767 holds the distance record for commercial twin-jet aircraft with a 9,253 mi. (14,890 km.) nonstop flight from Seattle, Wash., to Nairobi, Kenya, on June 12, 1990, in 17 hours 51 minutes.

A New York Helicopter Sikorsky S-58T takes off against the backdrop of the roof of the Trans World Airlines terminal. The helicopter service brings passengers from Manhattan's 34th street heliport and can carry up to 14 passengers.

Photo was taken from outside the center parking area near the Trans World Airlines terminal. The airline actually has two terminals: 4A serves international passengers, while 4B is for domestic flights. TWA commissioned Eero Saarinen, the Finnish-American architect, to design its terminal in 1956. Saarinen broke away from the rectilinear and unadorned "international style" that was favored then for most commercial public buildings. Instead, the two cantilevered, wing-like concrete shells forming the roof were a symbol of flight. Inside, curving pillars, supports and stairways recall the lines of the Art Nouveau style.

A 747-200B lands with flaps extended. Sabena operates two 747-200 and one -300 model. Several 747s were ordered by governments for VIP transport. The new Air Force One for the U.S. President is an example is a specially fitted -200B similar to the command post E-4B NEACAP. Several former airline 747SP have been converted for the same purpose for Middle-Eastern heads of state.

The control tower is the nerve center of the airport. The new tower can be seen from the end of runway 22R flanked by an ELAL 747-200 and Air Afrique DC-10-30. Air traffic control is a highly automated process. Towers at airports are the headquarters for local control. Responsibilities are divided among controllers who separate traffic on the ground from the aircraft on approach and those taking off. At Kennedy controllers may direct thousands of aircraft movements a day, more than one a minute during the busiest hours.

The old control tower, near the International terminal, is shown. Controllers in the visual control room at the top are responsible for aircraft taking off, for aircraft taxiing and for final landing instructions. Assistants log aircraft departures and arrival times. A ground movement planning controller books slots (available times) along the airways for departures.

A Boeing 747-200 of Iberia on approach to Runway 31R. On landing there is one sound that all pilots want to hear. That is the "thrump-thrump" of the landing gears or undercarriage locking into position. The powered glide to the ground follows with a greater sense of security. A safe separation distance of three or four miles between incoming flights provides a landing interval of about one minute. Aircraft overflying the congested airport zone are controlled by a separate radar director.

A 747-400 lands at about 175 mph. (285 kph.), a speed that is similar to other subsonic jets such as the McDonnell Douglas DC-10 and Lockheed 1011. The supersonic Concorde lands at 187 mph. (300 kph.).

A MD-11 of Finnair landing. The cockpit of the MD-11 is equipped with modern digital electronics. The aircraft's predecessor, the DC-10's cockpit was designed for a three-man crew, the MD-11 is flown by two people. The MD-11 is designed to carry 250 to 405 passengers, and caries a medium load of 322 passengers 7,920 miles.

pproach and landing on Runway 22L is viewed from the cockpit
a 747 arriving from Europe. Flight deck of the 747-400 is much
ss cluttered than the older 747 layout, due to completely new
ionics. The most noticeable difference between new and old is
e presence in the -400 of color television type screens, duplicat-
l to present information to both the pilot and copilot.

At the moment the tires touch the runway they begin revolving from 0 to 170 mph. The result: a large puff of burned rubber. Passengers have become familiar with the sudden burst of noise shortly after touchdown as the pilot opens the engines to reverse thrust, to help slow the aircraft.

Pan Am Express used to operate ten De Havilland Canada DHC-7-102 Dash 7 commuter aircraft to feed traffic to their long range flights. The airline is now owned by Trans World Express. The DHC-7 is powered by 4 Pratt & Whitney PT6A turboprop engines. This engine is very popular among small aircraft manufacturers.

The Polish flag carrier LOT used to operate Ilyushin IL-62M aircraft to Kennedy, now it has Boeing 767-200ER or -300ER aircraft for non-stop service between Warsaw and New York. The Boeing 767 and other large twin-jets land at about 155 mph. (254 kph.). The 767 was the first Boeing airplane to replace aluminum with graphite and Kevlar composites, which are lighter, stronger materials. The weight savings gained contribute to overall operating efficiency. This aircraft has replaced some of the older long-range three- and four-engine jets for Atlantic crossings.

ATR-42 commuter aircraft has been very popular with commuter and regional carriers who provide feed to international airlines. This ATR-42-300 registered N4209G carries 44 passengers was the 9th one delivered to Trans World Express.

British Airways terminal is shown from the air with the TWA terminals on top. The Concorde can be seen at a gate near a 747. A Concorde speed record was achieved on Dec. 30, 1985, when tail winds helped Concorde reach 1,490 mph. between New York and London, exceeding the previous record of 1,470 mph. Concorde's cruising speed is Mach 2 (1,350 mph.).

United Airlines' 747-400s are powered by four Pratt & Whitney PW4056 engines. The most powerful varient of the -400 built to date is with four Rolls-Royce RB211-524H engines producing over 240,000 lb. of thrust at takeoff. The 747-400 provides two-deck seating. The -300 introduced the stretched upper deck. United introduced 747 service in 1970.

Air India 747 landing on Runway 13L located in front of the British Airways terminal. The airline provides service to India via London with 747-200, -300 Combi and -400 aircraft.

Incoming Concorde from Paris can be seen on the runway 13L from the cockpit of Concorde G-BOAB departing for London. Supersonic aircraft must be slender, and the cabin of the Concorde is only 8 feet 8 inches wide. However, the aircraft is 204 feet long. Normal seating is for 100 passengers. Although the wingspan is less than 84 feet, fuel capacity is over 31,000 U.S. gallons.

Concorde taking off on Runway 22R and flying straight to the
Atlantic Ocean. Concorde has an initial rate of climb of 5,000
ft./min. (25.2 m./sec.). It usually reaches Mach 1 at 32,000 ft.
(9,500 m.) and Mach 2 at 50,000 ft. (16,600 m.) about 40 min.
after takeoff. The supersonic Concorde cruises between
52,000 and 59,000 feet, which allows the passenger to see
plainly the curvature of the earth on a clear day.

Aer Lingus 747 on the taxiways near 22R. The airline operates 747-100 air-craft across the North Atlantic. Some models of this aircraft have been oper-ated for more than two decades. Over the years there have been a number of increases in the maximum permitted weights of the basic 747-200, along with the introduction of more powerful engines.

DC-10-30 of Nigeria Airways landing on 13L. The DC-10-30's typical landing speed is 168 mph. (272 kph.) at a maximum weight of 403,000 lb. (182,800 kg.). The airline operated also 707-300C, 737-200 and A310-200 aircraft. All Nigeria operation are now suspended and some aircraft have been impounded and repossessed.

British Airways 767-300ER taxiing to its gate. British Airways was one of
the customers outside the U.S. and Japan to buy this aircraft and
specified that its 767s be fitted with Rolls-Royce RB211-524H engines
uprated to 60,600 lb. thrust. The 767 shares many design features with the
Airbus A300, though the 767 has a bigger wing and a narrower body.

A Northwest Cargo 747-251F, registered N640US. Parked near the cargo area along Runway 13L/31R and hangar 1 and 2, first hangars at the airport built in 1947. With the advent of the 747-200F in the early 1970s, air cargo became a very automated and efficient means of shipping large freight. Both loading and unloading are heavily automated and can be done by just a few men.

A DC-10-30F shown here in Federal Express colors undergoing a technical check. It was the final version of the DC-10 manufactured. McDonnell Douglas launched the DC-10 on Feb. 19, 1968, after receiving an order for the aircraft from American Airlines. Full production was launched in April of that year, when United Airlines also placed an order. The configuration and size of the DC-10 closely match those of the L-1011 TriStar, which Lockheed launched in March, 1968.

Northwest Airlines operates over six Boeing 747-251F pure freighter aircraft powered by Pratt & Whitney JT9–7F, –7Q and –7R4G2 turbofans.
The freighter is easy to recognize because it has no windows along the sides of the fuselage except for those on the short upper deck.

A Federal Express 747-200F takes off from Runway 13L. Most of the 747-100F and -200F operated were acquired during the purchase of Flying Tigers. Federal is in the process of selling all its 747 aircraft. The 747-100F freighter aircraft are converted from passenger use, many 747-100s have been converted to pure freighter versions by Boeing and other companies. The main change is the removal of all passenger-related equipment and the addition of a large side cargo door on the rear left.

pan Airlines 747-246F taking off. This version of the 747F is powered by ratt & Whitney JT9D-7Q and has a maximum take off weight of 820,000 . (372,000 kg). 747-200F freighter and 747-200C convertible are one of e only few civilian aircraft in the world with a fully opening nose to allow argo to be loaded from the front. These aircraft retain the rear left cargo oors and lower access doors on the belly. Both have a maximum lifting apacity of 250,000 lb. (113,600 kg.). Boeing recently launched its latest ersion of the 747-400, the -400F. This aircraft, like the -200F, has no pas- enger accommodations. It can lift over 250,000 lb. and has a range of ore than 6,500 mi. (10,000 km.).

Approach lights guide the aircraft to the threshold. A 747 is about to pass over the lead in lights on its way to Runway 13L. In today's aviation environment, aircraft begin their approaches to airports as far as 60 miles out. Coming from many directions, the aircraft are lined up by air traffic control, their speed is ordered and their descent carefully watched. Incoming traffic to runway 13L/31R sometimes finds commuter and large wide-body transports are stacked back to back. Most of the latest models of the large commercial jets are equipped with numerous electronic aids designed to provide fully automatic landings if needed.

Rich International Airways operates DC-8-62 aircraft for charters out of Miami and also flies Lockheed L-1011-1. Its DC-8 are powered by Pratt & Whitney JT3D-3B and -7 with "hush kits". The aircraft is remarkable in that it was built to two safety standards: fail-safe and fatigue-resistant. The DC-8 was one of the first commercial aircraft to use titanium for strength and weight savings.

Air France 747-200F landing, the airline operates one of the largest fleets of 747F dedicated freighters. Air France cargo area is in the second cargo section of the airport. It is located across from Runway 13L/31R and the American Airlines terminal. JFK in 1991 ranked first among U.S. airports in revenue cargo carried, with 1.385 million short tons, which was almost 5% less than cargo shipped from the airport the year before, due to the recession. By comparison, in 1991 Los Angeles International was second in revenue cargo, with 1.257 million short tons.

was purchased by Air France, so all
are now part of the Air France Cargo
747-200F rear and front cargo doors are
ading. The same cargo door is found in
erted 747-100s and all of the 747 Combi
Convertible models. It is loaded with
natic equipment operated by one man.
whole system is extremely efficient and
dient. The size and scale of the front
door of the 747F can be seen. The
g operation is done by one man, from
side.

A 747-200F of Air France with its large nose door open. Most large aircraft have front and rear cargo loading doors, but only a few have front loading capability. The procedure is fully automated and usually done by two people. Cargo revenues represent up to 20% of and airline's yearly sales.

e A340 landing on Runway 13L with its
ormous wings. The A340 shares its
sign with the A330, the only visible dif-
ence being deletion of the two outer
gines of the A340. The wings have
ward winglets similar to the 747-400.
e A340 cockpit resembles that of an
20 in outward appearance. The most
 portant differences are the advanced
ht management and navigation sys-
ns and controls for four engines instead
wo.

is Lufthansa A310-304, D-AIBF was the
            6th delivered to the airline.

The McDonnell-Douglas MD-11 operated by American is an improved version of the DC-10-30. Aerodynamic improvements of the MD-11 over the DC-10 include winglets and redesigned wing trailing edge, a smaller horizontal tail with integral fuel tanks and an extended tail cone. Three General Electric, Pratt & Whitney or Rolls-Royce engines power the MD-11. Another important feature is the new two-man digital "glass" cockpit.

American Airlines terminal is seen from the air in the morning, when most of the traffic is destined for other U.S. cities and the Caribbean. Commuter airliners bringing passengers for international destinations can be seen next to the DC-10s and A300s.

The evening Concorde inbound from London on approach to runway 13L/31R. Concorde does not have the same hours as subsonic flights; it flies mainly in the morning and at noon. Passengers describe the supersonic ride as exhilerating. For transatlantic blue-ribbon passengers, Concorde wipes out jet lag.

American Airlines uses the A300-600R on its Caribbean routes from Kennedy. The Airbus has the look of economic practicality about it. Designers put two pilots in the cockpit instead of three and hung two engines under the wings. The A300-600 borrowed from the A310 the two-man cockpit, tail fuel tank, wingtip fences, carbon brakes and composite materials.

The A300 fuel loading and forward freight door system is shown. The A300-600 is highly automated, enabling one man to do each job. The utility of Airbus aircraft is emphasized in its use of LD2 containers, commonly accepted cargo containers, and a special cargo loading system.

Shown from the air a TWA 747 rotates
on runway 13R, with a Tower Air 747
docked at the gate loading passengers at Terminal One, with morning
apron traffic. Runway 13R/31L is situ-
ated in front of Terminal 1A and One.
Terminal 1A is used by Delta and One
by Tower Air and charter operators.

A Port Authority car near
runway 13R/31L checking for birds
and debris on the runway to provide
for safe aircraft in traffic.

A300B4-200 of Air Jamaica on a landing roll with spoilers extended on Runway 13L. Now defunct, Eastern introduced the Airbus A300 into U.S. service. The Airbus Industrie consortium is composed of Aerospatiale in France, Deutsche Aerospace in Germany, British Aerospace, and CASA in Spain. Fokker of the Netherlands is an associate in the company.

Two 747-200 docked at Terminal One and 1A. Northwest no longer uses Terminal 1A or Terminal 3 but the International Arrivals building since 1933. The -200 has been the most popular version of the 747 series, but is no longer manufactured. The final -200 was delivered in November, 1991. The -200 version was certificated on Dec. 23, 1970, and was put into service by KLM Royal Dutch Airlines early in 1971.

An Eastern L1011-1 taxiing to runway 13R/31L during the winter of 1985. The airline has since ceased operations. L1011's are powered only by Rolls-Royce RB211 turbofans. The rear engine mounting is similar to the mounting on a Boeing 727. The inlet hole can be seen just above the aft fuselage. An S-duct links with the engine, which exhausts at the tail one.

elta L-1011 landing on runway 13R/31L. The L-1011 became the
commercial production aircraft of the Lockheed Corporation.
y models have been in service for over two decades.

A Boeing 757-200 operated by
Avensa of Venezuela, the airline also
flies DC-9-51, 737-200, 727-100 and -
200 aircraft.

The general aviation area is shown with a Gulfstream 3 business jet awaiting its VIP passengers. The Gulfstream G3 and G4 are the Rolls-Royce of business jets. They have a maximum take off weight of about 68,000 lb (31,000 kg) very close to the weight of a small DC-9-10 or a large commuter plane. they are powered by Rolls Royce Spey turbofans.

A Lockheed four-engined Jetstar II of the H. J. Heinz Corporation in "Ketchup" colors is on the taxiways near Runway 22L/R. The aircraft was produced in the 1960's as a business jet and also was bought by the U.S. Air force for VIP transport and designated the VC-140B and are powered by four Pratt & Whitney JT12A-8 turbojets.

Many of the world's 727 airliners have been converted to luxurious private or corporate jets. The most popular has been the 727-100. The three engine capability gives trans-oceanic range with great safety with the comfort of a wide cabin. Other popular uses for this aircraft type are as a testbed or as military VIP or transports.

Newark International

Opened on Oct. 1, 1928, Newark Airport was built on 68 acres of swampland and quickly became the world's busiest airport. As the first to serve the New York and New Jersey area, it has always been in the forefront of developments, being equipped at an early stage with paved runways, a weather bureau, night lighting and an Air Traffic Control center.

The airport is about 16 miles from midtown Manhattan—the same distance as JFK is from midtown. The airport currently consists of 2,300 acres, 880 acres of which were acquired after 1948, when the Port Authority of New York and New Jersey began operation of the airport.

The City of Newark spent about $8.2 million on construction and development of the airport; the U.S. government spent more than $15 million prior to 1948. By year-end 1992, the Port Authority of New York and New Jersey had invested $1 billion in the facility.

Newark witnessed many historic events during the pioneering years, including the inaugural coast-to-coast service in 1930 operated by a Ford Trimotor under the command of Charles Lindbergh.

During World War 2 the airport was acquired by the U.S. Army Air Corps, but in 1948 control passed to the Port Authority of New York under a lease from the City of Newark. The new operator quickly added an instrument runway, a new terminal building and cargo center, but traffic continued to grow dramatically during the 1950s, so plans were made for a major reconstruction of the facilities.

Almost immediately after the details were announced in 1964, work commenced on a new terminal complex, an additional runway and a vast expansion of the parking areas. Nevertheless, it was 1970 before the first of the improvements was ready for service. The other improvements followed during the next two years or so. In 1972, the airport officially became Newark International.

With the two terminal buildings A and B in use, the previous congestion was greatly reduced. However, after airline deregulation in the late 1970s, a large number of new carriers threatened to swamp the facilities.

One of the newcomers was People Express, which introduced frequent, low-cost services from Newark. However, the company took over the original north terminal building for its exclusive use, as the rental was much less than accommodations in the central area.

The authorities decided that it was time for major expansion, so Terminal C shell was built in 1972 and interior completed by 1988. Once it was operational, attention was turned to bringing Terminal B into use for international arrivals after years of being devoted to domestic movements. International arrivals were in Terminal C from 1984 until 1989. The task was completed in 112 days. The North Terminal area buildings were earmarked for conversion into a cargo and office complex.

There are three buildings known as terminal A, B and C. The first two branch out to three circular satellites, while the third has two concourses projecting from the main section. All terminals offer all amenities.

In the future, a monorail system will whisk passengers between terminals and long-term parking lots. Contracts for the system were completed in 1992, and passenger service is expected to start in 1995. The airport provides 21,000 parking spaces, more than 18,000 of them for the public.

Work has begun on a $110-million project to expand international passenger facilities in Terminal B and to construct a new international arrivals terminal on the ramp between the B-2 and B-3 connectors. The new facility will be capable of processing 3,000 arriving passengers an hour, and will increase the number of gates for wide-body aircraft to 14.

An MD-80 of American turning just off Runway 4R with the Empire State Building on the left. This runway runs along the New Jersey Turnpike and its sister runway 4L.

The skyline of lower Manhattan can be seen from an Airbus A310-300 taking off from funway 4L. The A310-300 with Pratt & Whitney JT9D engines was certificated by the French and West Germans on December 5, 1985, and service by Swissair began later that month. The A310 was the first Western aircraft to be given Russian State Aviation certification, in October, 1991.

Newark's tower with a DC-10 of Continental. The DC-10 cockpit was designed for a three-man crew. The DC-10 is powered with three General Electric CF6-50 engines. The center (no. 2) engine is mounted throught the base of the DC-10 tail. Rear engine mounting is unusual in the DC-10. The engine is integrated with the tail fin, held there like a large cigar.

Balair, the Swiss charter airline used to operate out of Kennedy, but now has weekly flights with A310-300 aircraft out of Newark. This A310 is powered by Pratt & Whitney PW4156A engines The A310-300 is available at maximum weights ranging from 330,000 to 361,600 lb. The first -300 version flew on July 8, 1985. The A310 is powered by Pratt & Whitney JT9D or PW4000 engines and the General Electric CF6-80.

USAir Fokker F-28 taking off. The airline operates F-28-1000 and -4000 series aircraft and the new improved version named the Fokker 100. All Fokker jets are powered by Rolls Royce Spey and Tay turbofans.

Delta MD-88 nearing its gate. The MD-88 is identical to the other MD-80 series aircraft except it has an electronic flight instruments system, windshear detection system and increased use of composites in the airframe. It was built specially for Delta Airlines. The MD-80 series borrowed from military technology the head-up displays in the cockpit.

An USAir Fokker F28 taxiing near Terminal A during the evening rush hour.

The world's largest transport aircraft, the Antonov An225 taking off on a flight
to deliver medical supplies to the children of Chernobyl. The maximum take
off weight of the modified version of the Antonov 124 Ruslan is 600,000 kg.
(1,320,000 lb.) and it is powered by six Lotarev D-18T turbofans.

United Express BAe 3200 Jetstream operated by Atlantic Coast Airlines.

United Parcel Service has important cargo operations across from
Terminal A in the cargo area next to Federal Express. This 747 registered
N676UP is a passenger 747-123 originally delivered to American Airlines
in 1970 and converted to an all cargo configuration 747-100F for UPS.
Most of the cargo traffic is at night.

Federal Express has a large cargo center for its fleet of MD-11, DC-10, 727 and Fokker F27 fleet of aircraft. This F27 friendship 500 aircraft used to be operated as a passenger aircraft by Malaysia Airlines and has been converted to all cargo for the overnight package carrier.

TAP Air Portugal operates out of Kennedy and Newark with its L-1011-500 and A310-300. Other smaller national airlines have done the same by switching airports in the recent years. Continental operates out of LaGuardia and Newark, but no longer out of Kennedy.

Miami Air operates ex-Eastern Airlines 727-200 Advanced aircraft to Florida. Smaller aircraft need less runway, typically 6,000 ft. (1,800 m), and are able to vacate the runway, rapidly to enable the other aircraft to land or take off. The much larger and heavier 757's need the same amount of runway as the smaller 727 or 737. The 757-200 typically lands at 150 mph. (245 kph).

An Airbus A300 just after a landing
run off Runway 4R taxiing to its
terminal. Continental operates
A300B4-100 and -200 aircraft,
mostly former Eastern aircraft powered by 2 General Electric CF6-50C2
powerplants.

Henson Airlines operates this
De Havilland DHC-8-100 Dash
8 for USAir Express.

Air Force One is the call name for the aircraft carrying the President of the United States. Two 747-200 repalce the 707-320B previously used. This 747-200B is specially outfitted with communications and other devices, in-flight refueling, and a large array of equipment to make self-sufficient. Four General Electric CF6-80C2B1 power the aircraft operated by the U.S. Air Force.

A Fokker F-28-1000 now operated by USAir since the ter's takeover of Piedmont Airlines. The F-28-1000 is wered by two Rolls Royce Spey 555-15P turbofans.

Northwest Airlink Fairchild SA227AC Metro 3 commuter aircraft at the gate at terminal A. The aircraft is operated by Northeast Express of Manchester, NH along with a fleet of Beechcraft 99 and Dash 8 aircraft.

Terminal C traffic.

Air Ontario operates mostly De Havilland DHC-8-100 aircraft like this one and a few Beechcraft 99 and one Convair 580. The airline is based in London, Ontario and provides commuter service to major North American hubs.

McDonnell Douglas DC-9-32 of Air Canada just after landing on runway 4L. Pilots love to fly this aircraft due to its "fighter aircraft" feel. This model is powered by Pratt & Whitney JT8-7A engines.

DC3 - tail of the cargo on the tarmac. Many former passenger or military DC-3's now carry freight all over the world.

LaGuardia

During the 1920s some of the site now covered by the airport was the home of the Gala Amusement Park. Transformed in 1929 into a 105-acre private flying field, it originally adopted the name Glenn H. Curtiss, but this was later changed to the North Beach Airport, a more appropriate name in view of its proximity to Flushing Bay and Bowery Bay. The airport now occupies about 650 acres. Of the three major airports serving New York City, LaGuardia is closest to midtown Manhattan—eight miles, its convenient location in the borough of Queens making it ideal for businessmen who want to be near

Manhattan. In the mid-1930s New York City took over the airport, and the city's enthusiastic Mayor Fiorello LaGuardia was mainly responsible for the facility's development as a businessmen's airport, a venture which was to prove highly suc-

cessful. Original construction by New York City came to $40 million. By the end of 1992 the Port Authority had invested almost $600 million in the airport.

Under new ownership in 1947, work commenced on enlarging the site by filling in 357 acres of waterfront along the east side. Construction then went ahead as a joint exercise of the City of New York and the federal Works Progress Administration, until on Oct. 15, 1939, all was ready for the opening ceremonies, followed by the first commercial services on Dec. 2. Mayor LaGuardia's contribution to the project was recognized in 1947 when his name was bestowed upon the airport, at the same time that control was transferred to the Port Authority.

The original building, known as the Overseas terminal, was located on the west side adjacent to the bay; a convenient spot for handling both flying boats and landplanes. While the need for this dual function has long gone, the structure is still used by commuter carriers and the Delta Washington and Boston shuttles. It also provides the airport's base for the regular water ferries to downtown Manhattan. It is now known as the Marine Air Terminal.

The Central Terminal Building (CTB) was opened on April 17, 1964 and serves most of the scheduled airlines. This impressive four-story structure has four two-level piers projecting from it, in total offering 38 aircraft gates. It is 1,300 ft.

sections at a cost of some $850,000. Airbus also modified the A300 landing gear.

Although there was sufficient capacity for many years, in March, 1981, the new Shuttle Terminal was opened to the public. At the same time the commuter traffic was temporarily relocated in the adjacent, but suitably modified, Hangar 8, until a further move was necessary, when the latter was earmarked for development.

long and 180 ft. wide, with 750,000 square feet of floor space.

From the outset the amount of land available was strictly limited, so four runways were laid originally. Although their length was adequate for the piston-engine aircraft in service in the early days, the demands of modern jets forced runways to be relocated or extended. Only runway 4/22 remains of the original four.

A major problem became apparent in the late 1970s, when Eastern Airlines announced its intention to introduce the Airbus A300 on its New York-Miami route. Although wide-body aircraft such as the McDonnell Douglas DC-10 and Lockheed L-1011 were being accommodated, it was feared that the new taxiways were not strong enough to withstand the different weight distribution of the European aircraft. Fortunately for Franco-American relations, the airport authorities agreed to strengthen the pier

Delta constructed its own facility at LaGuardia. Its complex entered service in June, 1983, at the eastern end of the airport. It has 10 aircraft gate positions. USAir opened its new $200-million terminal on September. 12, 1992. The 12-gate terminal is connected to the USAir Shuttle Terminal and has about 300,000 square feet of floor space.

The expanded arrivals area of the CTB was opened for use on Oct. 1, 1992. The 56,000 square foot expansion provides a much-enlarged common circulation corridor and adds exclusive baggage claim space to each airline's baggage claim area. In 1993 redevelopment of the center section of the CTB was begun. The project will create a spectacular concession environment, including new retail stores and a food court.

The New York skyline with a USAir 737-300 in
the foreground. The airlines operates 737-200, -
300 and -400 aircraft as well as the former Trump
Shuttle 727-200's.

The famous control tower at LaGuardia can be seen with a DC-9-31 on a takeoff roll on runway 4. DC-9s are powered by Pratt & Whitney JT8D engines. The DC-9 has rear-mounted engines, just like the Caravelle. One reason for positioning them there was to keep noise from most of passenger cabin. Short-range, low-capacity transports soon gave way to stretched versions.

A320-211 of Northwest taking off on Runway 13. Northwest was among the first airlines in North America to order the Airbus A320. Its high technology and fuel efficiency make the aircraft an attractive replacement for the Boeing 727. Typical of contemporary commercial aircraft, the A320 is flown by a two-person cockpit crew.

sh hour line up along Runway 13/31. United, USAir and Delta
the three of the major competitors at LaGuardia along with
erican.

Shorts 330-100 commuter aircraft approaching runway 31.
The SD330 is powered by two Pratt & Whitney Canada
PT6A-45A turboprop engines. American Eagle is based in
Dallas and operates a very large fleet of commuter aircraft.

Traffic in front of the Central Terminal Building can be seen. A clear view
is available from the roof of the building. A United 727 taxiing along runway 13/31 and at the gate are the 727 aircraft of now defunct Pan Am
and thrice defunct Braniff.

A 737-300 of United lands on runway 22 during the late afternoon rush-hour. The CFM56 engine powers the more recent versions of the 737 such as the dash 300, 400 and 500 series. It became the aircraft of choice after deregulation, airlines appreciating its two-person crew and two-engine economies.

An Allegheny Commuter Airlines aircraft landing. The commuter airline is part of the USAir Express network to feed passengers to USAir.

The USAir terminal.

MD-80 landing on Runway 22. The MD-80 series owes its origin to the DC-9. The twin-engine, two-crew member DC-9 was a desirable aircraft for high-frequency, low-cost trips under U.S. airline deregulation.

An Airbus A320 taking off from runway 13. The A320-100 was offered originally, but was replaced from late 1988 by the -200, which has wingtip fences, a wing center-section fuel tank and a higher takeoff weight.

New York Air DC-9-30 landing on runway 31 in 1985. The airline was launched by Texas Air to provide low cost flights to Washington and Boston and was later made part of Continental.

7-251 of Northwest taxiing near the main terminal still painted in the
d livery of the airline. This version is powered by Pratt & Whitney PW2037
gines.

F28-4000 approaching Runway 31. The F28 is highly maneuverable in flight. It was designed with a wing sweepback of only 16 degrees, for good handling at low speed. During landings the F28 brake system involves the whole tail breaking out and increases drag.

DC-9-31 taking off from runway 31. This aircraft registered N1799U was originally owned by Republic Airlines and is now part of Northwest's fleet since its takeover of Republic.

Eastern was the first operator of
A300s in the U.S. This short range
A300B2-K3C was used on shuttle
operations.

Private and corporate aircraft are often present in LaGuardia. This Canadair CL-601 has been the basis for a recent version stretched to carry 50 passengers over short distances called Regional Jet.

A Delta 767-300 taxiing with the 1964 world's fair site can be seen in the background. The airline operates 767-200, -300 and -300ER extended range versions of the aircraft. The extended-range capabilities of the Boeing 767 were recognized by airlines. Aviation authorities have worked out a set of precautions for operators to take. These include the operation of an on-board auxiliary power unit to maintain systems in the case of an engine shutdown, cooling apparatus for computers, and additional fire extinguishers for the cargo hold.

Ransome De havilland DHC-7-102 Dash 7 landing. This commuter airline based in Philadelphia was part of the "Delta Connection" in the early 1980's. Later it became Pan Am Express and again was sold to Trans World Express. this aircraft still retains it original registration N171RA.

...idwest Express provides feeder connection at major hubs with ...C-9-32 aircraft like this one and smaller -14 or -15 versions ...cquired from other airlines. It also operates MD-88 aircraft.

John F. Kennedy International Airport

Movements (000):	1992	1991	1990	1989	1988
Total Aircraft	321	277	303	305	304
Total Passengers	27,800	26,200	29,800	30,300	31,200
Cargo Tonnage	1,400	1,300	1,300	1,400	1,300

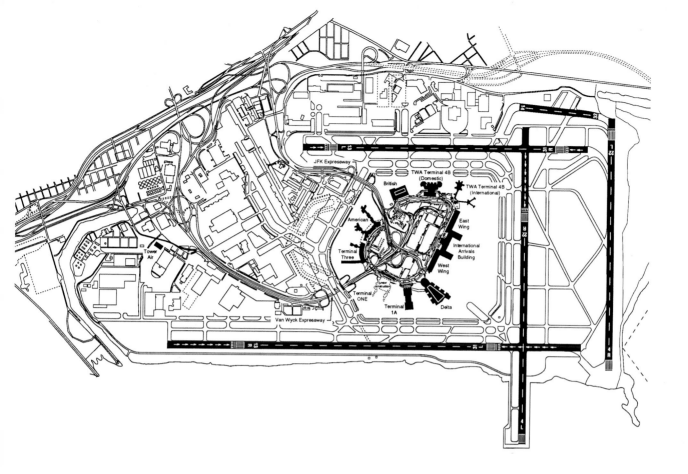

Runways:
The runway system consists of two pairs of parallel runways.Total runway length is nine miles (14.5 km) All runways have high intensity runway edge lighting, centerline and taxiway exit lighting, and are grooved to improve skid resistance and minimize hydroplaning.

Length	feet	meters
4L-22R	11,351	3,460
4R-22L	8,400	2,560
13L-31R	10,000	3,048
13R-31L	14,572	4,442

Taxiways:
A total of 22 miles (35.6 km) in length. Standard width is 75 feet (25 m), with 25 foot heavy duty shoulders and 25 foot erosion control pavement on each side. the taxiway centerline light system has largely displaced the edge light system previously used. Taxiways are generally of asphaltic concrete or line, cement, flyash composition 15 to 18 inches thick. A sign system, illuminated at night provides directional information for taxiing aircraft.

Radio frequencies (Mhz):
Tower	119.1	123.9
Approach	132.4	
Departure	135.9	
Ground	121.65	121.9

Newark International Airport

Movements (000):	1992	1991	1990	1989	1988
Total Aircraft	410	378	379	365	370
Total Passengers	24,300	22,300	22,200	20,900	22,500
Cargo Tonnage	577	473	495	441	449

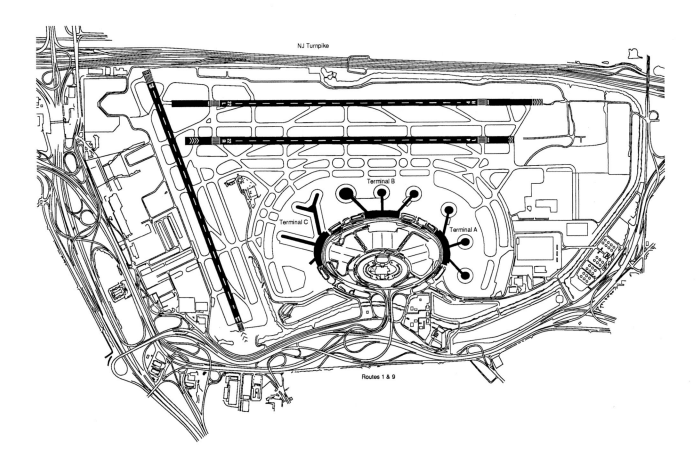

NJ Turnpike

Terminal B

Terminal C

Terminal A

Routes 1 & 9

Runways:

The runway system consists of two parallel runways and a third runway 11-29 which is primarily used for commuter traffic. Runway 4R landings can be permitted with visibility of less than a quarter mile (400 m) and on 4L landings allowed only with half mile visibility. Both runways have displaced thresholds to minimize noise effects. High intensity runway edge and centerline, as well as high speed exit taxiway centerline lighting on taxiways complete the visual aids package.

Runway	feet	meters
4L-22R	8,200	2,499
4R-22L	9,300	2,835
11-29	6,800	2,072

Taxiways:

More than 12 miles (19.4 km) of 75 foot (25 m) wide taxiways, entirely equipped with centerline lighting, link the three runways with the central terminal and cargo areas. taxiways also have erosion pavement on each side.

Radio frequencies (Mhz):		
Tower	118.3	134.05
Departure	119.2	
Ground	121.8	126.15

LaGuardia Airport

Movements (000):	1992	1991	1990	1989	1988
Total Air Transport	324	324	356	349	362
Total Passengers	19,700	19,700	22,800	23,200	24,200
Cargo Tonnage	55	66	70	63	56

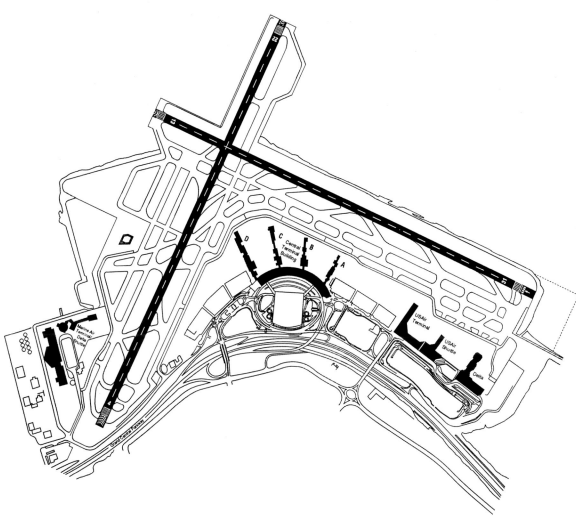

Runways:

The runway system consists of two runways. In a project completed in 1967 both runways were extended to 7,000 feet. The extensions were built on a 50 acre, L-shaped pile-supported concrete structure. The northerly 2,000 feet extension to runway 4-22, complete with taxiway and holding pad, was built into the Rickers Island Channel and opened to air traffic March 1966. Similarly, the westerly 13-31, with parallel taxiway, was extended in the Channel and opened in November 1966. Two 3,000 foot piers were constructed beyond the ends of the runway extensions to support Approach Lighting System with sequenced flashers.

Runway	Feet	Meters
4-22	7,000	2,134
13-31	7,000	2,134

Taxiways:

All taxiways are equipped with centerline lights except for taxiways Y, AC and R (between Runway 22 and 13). Nine additional aircraft parking spaces have been constructed at the end of Taxiway E.

Radio frequencies (Mhz):

Tower	118.7
Approach	120.8
Departure	120.4
Ground	121.7

New York Region
JFK, EWR, LGA and Teterboro airports

Movements (000):	1992	1991	1990	1989	1988
Total Aircraft	1,057	980	1,039	1,019	1,036
Total Passenger	71,700	68,200	74,800	74,400	77,800
Cargo Tonnage	1,900	1,800	1,900	1,900	1,800

World Airports

Passengers carried (000)	1991
Chicago's O'Hare International	59,257
Dallas-Fort Worth	48,198
Los Angeles International	45,668
Tokyo International (Haneda)	42,015
London Heathrow	40,495
Atlanta Hartsfield	37,915
San Francisco International	31,774
Denver Stapleton International	28,285
Frankfurt International	27,978
JFK International	27,441
Miami International	26,591
Osaka International	23,483
Paris Orly	23,320
Newark International	23,055
Honolulu International	22,224
Boston Logan	21,547
Minnesota St. Paul	20,601
LaGuardia	20,545

Notes for all data:
Total Aircraft movements is for international and domestic scheduled passenger, charter, cargo, commuter and non-revenue, including air taxi, business and private, government and helicopters.

Total Passenger movements is for international and domestic scheduled passenger, charter and commuter traffic.

Cargo Tonnage movements is for international and domestic cargo in short tons for revenue freight.